PUT ON YOUR GLASSES AND DRINK FROM A GLASS

TRICKY, STICKY WORDS

By STEPHEN O'CONOR
Illustrations by ANNABEL TEMPEST
Music by DREW TEMPERANTE

CANTATA
LEARNING

WWW.CANTATALEARNING.COM

CANTATA
LEARNING

Published by Cantata Learning
1710 Roe Crest Drive
North Mankato, MN 56003
www.cantatalearning.com

A note to educators and librarians from the publisher: Cantata Learning has provided the following data to assist in book processing and suggested use of Cantata Learning product.

Publisher's Cataloging-in-Publication Data
Prepared by Librarian Consultant: Ann-Marie Begnaud
Library of Congress Control Number: 2016938090
    Put on Your Glasses and Drink from a Glass : Tricky, Sticky Words
    Series: Read, Sing, Learn
    By Stephen O'Conor
    Illustrations by Annabel Tempest
    Music by Drew Temperante
    Summary: Learn about homonyms, words that are spelled the same but have different meanings, in this playful song.
    ISBN: 978-1-63290-797-4 (library binding/CD)
Suggested Dewey and Subject Headings:
    Dewey: E 428.1
    LCSH Subject Headings: Homonyms – Juvenile literature. | Homonyms – Songs and music – Texts. | Homonyms – Juvenile sound recordings.
    Sears Subject Headings: English language – Homonyms. | School songbooks. | Children's songs. | Popular music.
    BISAC Subject Headings: JUVENILE NONFICTION / Language Arts / Vocabulary & Spelling. | JUVENILE NONFICTION / Music / Songbooks.

Book design and art direction: Tim Palin Creative
Editorial direction: Flat Sole Studio
Music direction: Elizabeth Draper
Music written and produced by Drew Temperante

Printed in the United States of America in North Mankato, Minnesota.
072017   0367CGF17

ACCESS THE MUSIC!

SCAN
CODE
WITH
MOBILE
APP

CANTATALEARNING.COM

TIPS TO SUPPORT LITERACY AT HOME

WHY READING AND SINGING WITH YOUR CHILD IS SO IMPORTANT

Daily reading with your child leads to increased academic achievement. Music and songs, specifically rhyming songs, are a fun and easy way to build early literacy and language development. Music skills correlate significantly with both phonological awareness and reading development. Singing helps build vocabulary and speech development. And reading and appreciating music together is a wonderful way to strengthen your relationship.

READ AND SING EVERY DAY!

TIPS FOR USING CANTATA LEARNING BOOKS AND SONGS DURING YOUR DAILY STORY TIME

1. As you sing and read, point out the different words on the page that rhyme. Suggest other words that rhyme.

2. Memorize simple rhymes such as Itsy Bitsy Spider and sing them together. This encourages comprehension skills and early literacy skills.

3. Use the questions in the back of each book to guide your singing and storytelling.

4. Read the included sheet music with your child while you listen to the song. How do the music notes correlate to the words of the song?

5. Sing along on the go and at home. Access music by scanning the QR code on each Cantata book. You can also stream or download the music for free to your computer, smartphone, or mobile device.

Devoting time to daily reading shows that you are available for your child. Together, you are building language, literacy, and listening skills.

Have fun reading and singing!

What comes to mind when you hear the word *glasses*? Do you think of something that helps people to see or things that hold drinks? Either way, you are correct! These words are homonyms. They are spelled the same but have different meanings.

Are there other tricky, sticky words? Find out by turning the page. Remember to sing along!

Listen very carefully. What do you hear?
Some little words can fool your ear!

Speak very carefully. What did you say?
Some little words you might not mean that way!

Shoes are heavy, but slippers feel *light*.
We turn on a *light*, so we can see at night.

Light or *light*,

which word is right for me?

Is it easy to lift?
Or do I flip a switch?
Listen carefully!

Listen very carefully. What do you hear?
Some little words can fool your ear!

Speak very carefully. What did you say?

Some little words you might not mean that way!

We use *scales* to see how much we weigh.

The *scales* on fish shine bright when they play.

Scales or *scales*,

which word is right for me?

How much have I grown?
Or what's in my fishbowl?
Listen carefully!

Listen very carefully. What do you hear?
Some little words can fool your ear!

Speak very carefully. What did you say?
Some little words you might not mean that way!

Glasses can help you see clearly.
Glasses hold water and milk for me.

Glasses or *glasses*,
which word is right for me?

Do I need help to see?

Or am I just thirsty?

Listen carefully!

Listen very carefully. What do you hear?
Some little words can fool your ear!

Speak very carefully. What did you say?
Some little words you might not mean that way!

I'm a *fan* of swimming in the swimming pool!
A *fan* spins around and keeps us cool.

Fan or *fan*,
which word is right for me?

Do I like something a lot
or need to cool off?
Listen carefully!

Listen very carefully. What do you hear?
Some little words can fool your ear!

SONG LYRICS
Put on Your Glasses and Drink from a Glass

Listen very carefully. What do
  you hear?
Some little words can fool your ear!
Speak very carefully. What did
  you say?
Some little words you might not
  mean that way!

Shoes are heavy, but slippers
  feel light.
We turn on a light, so we can see
  at night.
Light or light,
which word is right for me?

Is it easy to lift?
Or do I flip a switch?
Listen carefully!

Listen very carefully. What do
  you hear?
Some little words can fool your ear!
Speak very carefully. What did
  you say?
Some little words you might not
  mean that way!

We use scales to see how much
  we weigh.
The scales on fish shine bright when
  they play.
Scales or scales,
which word is right for me?

How much have I grown?
Or what's in my fishbowl?
Listen carefully!

Listen very carefully. What do
  you hear?
Some little words can fool your ear!
Speak very carefully. What did
  you say?
Some little words you might not
  mean that way!

Glasses can help you see clearly.
Glasses hold water and milk for me.
Glasses or glasses,
which word is right for me?

Do I need help to see?
Or am I just thirsty?
Listen carefully!

Listen very carefully. What do
  you hear?
Some little words can fool your ear!
Speak very carefully. What did
  you say?
Some little words you might not
  mean that way!

I'm a fan of swimming in the
  swimming pool!
A fan spins around and keeps
  us cool.
Fan or fan,
which word is right for me?

Do I like something a lot
or need to cool off?
Listen carefully!

Listen very carefully. What do
  you hear?
Some little words can fool your ear!

Put on Your Glasses and Drink from a Glass

Hip Hop
Drew Temperante

Chorus

Lis - ten ver - y care - ful - ly. What do you hear? Some lit - tle words can fool your ear! Speak ver - y care - ful - ly. What did you say? Some lit - tle words you might not mean that way!

Verse

1. Shoes are heav - y, but slip-pers feel light. We turn on a light, so we can see at night. Light or light, which word is right for me? Is it eas - y to lift? Or do I flip a switch? Lis-ten care - ful-ly!

Chorus

Verse 2
We use scales to see how much we weigh.
The scales on fish shine bright when they play.
Scales or scales,
which word is right for me?
How much have I grown?
Or what's in my fishbowl?
Listen carefully!

Chorus

Verse 3
Glasses can help you see clearly.
Glasses hold water and milk for me.
Glasses or glasses,
which word is right for me?
Do I need help to see?
Or am I just thirsty?
Listen carefully!

Chorus

Verse 4
I'm a fan of swimming in the swimming pool!
A fan spins around and keeps us cool.
Fan or fan,
which word is right for me?
Do I like something a lot
or need to cool off?
Listen carefully!

Outro

Lis - ten ver - y care - ful - ly. What do you hear? Some lit - tle words can fool your ear!

23

GLOSSARY

Homonyms

fan—a machine with blades that spin to cool the air

fan—a person who loves something, usually an activity, a team, or a place

glasses—eyewear that helps people see

glasses—things you drink out of

light—something that shines and lets you see in the dark

light—not heavy

scales—tools that people use to weigh themselves

scales—the overlapping pieces that protect a fish's skin

GUIDED READING ACTIVITIES

1. Homonyms are words that are spelled the same but have different meanings. What are two meanings for *second*, *story*, *duck*, and *letter*?

2. Play the song again. Each time you hear the word *listen*, cup your ears. Can you think of any other dance moves for this song?

3. Make up a silly story that uses all four homonym pairs in this book: light/light, scales/scales, glasses/glasses, and fan/fan. You can write your story or say it out loud.

TO LEARN MORE

Adamson, Thomas K., and Heather Adamson. *How Do You Measure Weight?* North Mankato, MN: Capstone, 2011.

Felix, Rebecca. *A Pair of Pears*. Mankato, MN: Amicus, 2015.

Murguia, Bethanie Deeney. *Cockatoo, Too*. New York: Little Bee Books, 2016.

Viva, Frank. *Outstanding in the Rain*. New York, Boston: Little, Brown and Company, 2015.